Persephone in a Motel Room

LANA RAFAELA CINDRIC

Cover art: Sneha Baste
Calligraphy: Natalia Kolodziej

Mythology references:
Hans Dieter Betz
William Smith
Cicero

ISBN: 9798665647647

Dedication

All of these are to me.

Acknowledgments

Before anyone else, I want to thank **my family** for their continuous support, even when I am running on coffee and frustration alone. Persephone wouldn't have been possible if you hadn't showed up and kept showing up for me. Thank you.

A huge thank you to **Natalia Kolodziej**, who knows my work, even when it feels like a stranger to me. Thank you for helping me turn a loose collection of poems into the story of my Persephone, with her cherries in place of pomegranates. And thank you for your beautiful calligraphy.

Thank you to **Sneha Baste**. Thank you for the stunning cover, and thank you for knowing what I wanted Persephone to feel like.

And thank you to **my grandmother**, who is no longer in this world, but will always remain with me. I know you couldn't understand English, but you always understood me.

I also want to thank my friends, readers, and supporters who made me take the plunge and turn some of my most personal poems into the book you are holding in your hands.

To **Anna Malacrida**, thank you for the sunshine. To **Shiloh Justice**, thank you for coining the words that found their way to this back cover. To **Sevval Yildirim**, thank you creating your beautiful art and inspiring me with every piece, poem, and conversation. To **Tay Hollingsworth**, thank you for your stunning support, and the daily dose of optimism. To **Sadie Abernathy**, thank you for your own poetry that makes me want to be better. To **Jessica Rabello**, who knows the borderline between sweetness and fury, and navigates it with phenomenal ease. To **Mitta Thakrar**, one of the first people who saw something in my poetry. To **Avery Sheridan**, thank you for your incredible light. To **Priya Chaudhary**, a book lover after my own heart. To **Zoha Jan,** thank you for your kindness and understanding. To **Farhah Mohd**, for her grace and lightness of heart that keeps inspiring me, day in and day out. To **Colleen Dunlap**, one of my first poetry friends. Give Charlie, Viktor, and Oliver a huge hug for me.

The only reason you found something special in my poetry is because *you* are special.

Finally, thank **you**. If you're reading this, I hope this story shows you that, yes, *This Is How You Survive* was about knowing that you can save yourself, but Persephone is all about feeding yourself first and loving every inch of the beautiful, dirty road.

Run wild!

Contents

You ever wake up feeling wanted?
Impossible warmth, down to your toes,
turning your belly into a pitcher,
pouring honey all over.

Room I

innocence

INNOCENCE

She grows up with two hearts in her chest.
One
sheltered,
the other as windswept as a plain.

Kore: ancient Greek, *maiden.*

"The seed of the fruits of the fields."

- Cicero -

The Greek Pantheon Is Drinking Rakija in My Grandmother's Kitchen

You wanna say we're cursed but fuck,
I'm feeling saved tonight.
Ten thousand metaphors for our ruin and destruction
and we're still going. I take comparison
like a blade to my throat / when the blood comes
I let it. It never turns into flowers
but I'd take stones, too. Another Olympus
topples to the ground & in my house in the Balkans
I've been taught not to give a fuck.

The Ruins After the Summer

in august the ruins after summer i am just pomegranate lust

I'll bring you cherries, you deserve sweetness.

Listen, I know that August summer is the heaviest kind of summer;
it either comes with sun licking at your throat or *feral*
dripping down your fingertips.

We drive and we drive, we look for nothing, we have

no one. Your knees are bruised and my heart is tired.
Listen, can't you see that this is not our fault?
These are the stars and the seat and the heat,

God, the heat - -
it might just drive me crazy.

Don't *you* turn wild,
don't *you* want to open your ribcage
and see what this darkness is made of?

In August, I am just pomegranate lust.

In August, you are just a long drive home when the sky
is the same shade of bruised as your knees.
You want me to tell you a pretty story and I have none
left up my sleeve. Mine all end with terror
and you want hope.

But there is hope in terror, I argue.

White-knuckled grip on the steering wheel,
don't look back don't think of home
leave it all behind, but all I see when I look out of my
window are the ruins after the summer.

Someone loved here and the graffiti
still carries the longing.
I bet the Coke can lying in the dirt tasted like heaven with
condensation slipping down slender fingertips. July was
just *kinder*.

August is desperate and I can see you looking at me now.
I've got precisely five freckles on my shoulder and now
you look like you're going to cry. God,
I never wanted for any of this to happen.
Two wretched things should amount to something whole,
but here we are.

There is no hope in terror. Tell me a pretty story.

Sometimes I want to scream until my lungs burst and
rip open my ribcage not for the darkness – but for the fury.
Like, look, world, look: this is what you made me become.
I've got a century's worth of rage and for fuck's sake,
I just wanted to *bloom*.

Sometimes when the heat is oppressive, we find ways
to cool down and your strawberry stained fingertips
remind me of hope. I carry it in my chest but the skies are
too dark. There will be no good luck charms in this story.
Keep carrying yours on your wrist, mine is six feet under.
Sometimes, in the dead of night,
when the world has forgotten about girls
with matches for fingers,
I think that I am capable of horrible things.

(Don't you know that nothing feels quite as good as
forgetting that you have a body
and melting into pure soul?)

That's not hope, that's madness.

Discarded sunscreen bottles stain my vision orange.
The sea is so, so far away.
We'll be wild by the time we come home
and we will have forgotten what it felt like to be
weightless.

But someone loved here,
someone cried here,
and someone saw the light here.

Why does it feel like mud now?

See, baby, all we have are these dreams,
nights painted purple and our bodies,
a little worse for the wear.
It makes for a really shitty scene,
two kids on their way to something,
just an empty tank and a miracle between them.

Do you still want a story? I'll give you one.
When I close my eyes, I am a sun stained ocean wave
crashing and crashing and finally, *I am infinite.*

When you close your eyes, I roll the windows down and
that's when you seem to smile. All I can see is the blue sea,
even miles into the mountains.
Our fingers never fit quite right and this is not
the kind of thing that people pull and find themselves in
history books.

But we have nothing to lose so in August,
I sleep with my windows open and my skin bare
and I am not a person,
you are not a person, we are two stray pieces of starstuff
mistaking Earth for a new home.

All we do is find ways to pass the time and devise ghosts
out of lonely places.

In August, pomegranate songs are the only things
rolling off our tongues.

In August, we learn that these bodies
carry traces of longing, they are cages
and we must learn how to grow. We find beauty
in the terror, we learn that, for all your hope,
for all my absence of it – we are just ruins
after the summer.

In September, I will tell you a pretty story.
I will make it so, so good for you.
I'll even let you lick it off my fingertips and call it nectar.

But it's August now so let me drive, won't you?
We will never get away but we might as well try.

Ribbon

You believe in ridiculous things,
tie a ribbon the color blue
around your wrist. You
are before all
a mosaic of broken rust
shin splinter glass door hurricane
outrage.
When you broke the glass over the
kitchen table
and pronounced yourself
an impossible
                    myth
did you cry out,
did you laugh.

Jimmy part I

Jimmy's got two hands and a stupid name
he doesn't let me call him by.
We sit in the parking lot and I watch him kill a bird
trying to teach it how to fly.
He asks me: *Am I good yet?*
Am I good -

Jimmy's got a crooked nose and a terrified heart,
he wants to be good so he tightens his grip when I
preach to him the benefits of sinning.
What are we going to be forgiven for
if we never did anything wrong?

Jimmy strains the limitations of physics, his belief
to be good pushing him to great heights.

I have never seen someone so hungry
for something so small.

Am I good, it fucks me up when I hear it
two feet in the river, two hands in the bloody pool,
he says: *I am good.*

I've got two hands and a stupid name
I love when he calls me by,
like how he wraps his tongue around
the letters, like I'm real, like we are not people
but bigger.

I've got a straight nose and a terrified heart.

We sit in the parking lot and cover my hands with dirt
when I try to teach him how to fly.

Lazy August

That August we lay low
lower than the fences
lower than the railings
a whole world rushing to live out there
and we wanted to be small.

Plastered ourselves to the parquet,
watched it breeze past,
your hand on your collarbone,
we were lazy.

You laughed like homemade iced tea,
drank on a porch somewhere
with nothing but cicadas
for violins.

That August we lay low
and observed our breathing,
the steady heartbeat thump,
inside our chests there was a bird
and we held it
best we could.

They said to take the rotting flowers
and throw them into the river
but we made crowns,
in the lazy August we dared not imagine
the absence of our fears.
They gave us everything we ever had.

Night Glo

I don't care, it feels like magic between my fingertips.

One of these days, you are going to wake up in the middle of the afternoon when the light hits you right, when the sunset pools over the horizon like an oil spill.

We are made of moments like these: listen, turn down the bass and listen. The ships are leaving and we always were port children; learned what sea salt was long before we even knew how to pronounce it.
Listen, no, I mean, actually *listen* because here is your skin and it's warm long after sundown, and here is your heart – this is a bird trapped in your chest. The ships are leaving and you must go with them.

Now the night glows around us but we're good. God knows these streets never loved us but we loved what we had, the fading glow, the pulsating heart under our bare feet. If I could bottle this feeling, I'd pick a vial and label it sugar sweet. If it killed me, I'd just laugh it off.

This summer left all of us with mouths full of gravel. I used to wake up angry but now I'm just coming home.

The darkest parts of us are suddenly illuminated and we do not know what to do with them; we do not know what fireworks are, we do not know what redemption is,

we know nothing except that we are a revelation away
from finding the truth.

We are still a prophet short but the fluorescent glow looks
like a beacon at last.

Chlorine Years

Chlorine years, press my mouth to your hair
and I can smell the pool, the emptied
wreck, the decay, trees
sprouting from the living room floor.

Matchstick years, wish I could say we burned
for nothing but we always burned for
something, the dreams, the schemes,
when they write our names in the history
it will be – sensible, sensible, what sensible
children.

Memory years, hope you don't mind me
taking these, shamelessly appropriating these
to make them better than they were, don't we all
lie in childhood, come on tell me one
good
lie,
I don't even care about the truth.

Your memories looked so unloved
on your porch and I am a fucking slut
for the cicadas,
the peach iced tea,
this shit peddled on TV that I could still feel,
which is life also.

I spent the night car-keying poetry
and I was hoping for thunder, was hoping
for a lightning strike on the eighth island -
they say it's a phantasm but I know better,
I know wishing enough makes it true;

I've been workin' on faith a long time
and when I am hungry,
I am hungry for everything.

Ode to Madness

Raised in the lap of passion borderline madness,
now you expect me to be *mild*.

Didn't you know that I am a supernova,
and this is a swan song, this is all just the calm
before the soulstorm?

I'm just sitting on my crazy,
waiting for the right moment,
tired of going through the motions,
I take a baseball bat to
life as I knew it.

Shit, I'd dance naked in the middle of the street
and all this -
this is just the countdown,
Lady Godiva sitting at the bottom of the swimming pool.

Because I was raised in the lap of the sounds of a violin,
a yearning
for different times, a crescendo that ends
with a war.

I was raised with history: look how we suffered,
look how we laughed, and how, even on the brink of war,
we were learning to love.

No one has ever taught me how to be mild.

I lived for everything I loved,
because I was raised in the lap of passion
and you don't forget the taste of freedom.

So if I die,
let me die
with my soul full of late night music
and coffee at midnight.

If I die like this,
I'll die laughing
with joy on my lips,
and stars in my eyes,
and no regrets.

No regrets.

The Women in My Family

The women in my family are
fucking rock stars,
you could never reach this level of cool.
Born-on-Tuesday fighters
seeing yourself in our reflective glasses,
the silver mirror is a pool.

I imagine we hold court again
at our kitchen table,
and the gifts they bring are not flour and gold -
in my family of women,
the kitchen is where we wage wars.

My Mother

My mother, an expert
in fucking shit up
in a good way, in a way that bites back
at the dogs trying to chase her.
My mother, a tree,
roots like nothing you'd ever seen,
refusing to be moved until *she* decides to.
My mother, a fast runner, a skillful climber, my
mother, the fearless, my mother, never giving up,
my mother and her four-poster-bed heart,
shaking and shaking until the world gives her
what she is owed.

My Grandmother and I

My grandmother and I, two peas in a pod,
squeezing our asses in the tight backseat, 14 hours,
my grandmother and I.

My grandmother and I, allies
always
moonlighting as experts at launching slippers
and exchanging gifts, my grandmother
and I, who forgot to translate poems
but said: "Here's your motivation to learn English"
to my grandmother,
who did not need to understand English to understand
what I have always been trying to say.

My grandmother and I, red nail polish and polished hair
with crumbling lives, always looking back
like some long lost royalty,
peering over their shoulders only to see their home
set ablaze. My grandmother and I,
experts in fucking shit up, experts in getting people
to say: "Oh, she's a hard one to contend with," my
grandmother and I, hard personalities, harder hearts,
still plenty of love to go around,
around the table full of food,
with hands capable of warmth,
and not many are.

My grandmother and I, smiling at the camera,
My grandmother and I, because we don't know how to do
anything else,
My grandmother and I, but to be happy,
My grandmother and I, because only the two of us know
what is behind us,
My grandmother and I, who know secrets,
My grandmother and I, who know recipes and prophecies,
My grandmother and I, that always came true.

My grandmother and I,
tight spaces, torn up places,
kitchen knife moments of bravery,
my grandmother and I,
the holy guardians
of all things fair.

The Garden

I dream of a garden,
right by the dusty road,
one bottle of Coke
spilling on the floor.

Oh, we'd hang sheets
over the windows when it's hot,
invent spells, the names of which
we forgot.

I dream of a garden
roses red like you've never seen,
holding court with all the women
in my family's seams.

Reading Tarot on a Broken Porch

Broken screen door, my hand on the wheel. So many birds died the year we chose to turn on the lights. We closed the door, tricked them into thinking we were the sky. Broken screen door, remember that you loved my blood first. And I'm just looking for someone with honest hands, a bottle of whiskey in the cabinet. I'm sorry for the blood on the floor. Broken screen door through which our children passed, my sense of humor, your curiosity. Golden. Golden. Broken screen door, my death was turning into the fool. The stars were telling me to leave, but I couldn't move. I was the entire scope of your deck, every card at once. And look, look how terrible you've made me. I've turned a loving house into a ruin for you. Broken screen door, the cracks keep showing up in the walls of us. One of these days, the wind is going to blow from the south and we'll be gone. Love is such a wicked thing when it rots. But leave it to me to be kneeling on the porch, collecting the glass. I'm the toast of a town that forgot my name but listen, I can spin this. If nothing, I am an expert at extracting gold from our rubble.

Hearts

The only thing I ruined my knees for
was trying to walk too quietly
shifting my weight in the dead of night
as if apologizing for being here,
for daring to make the noise that living things make.

Things come back to me now. Things like my reflection
two years back,
things which never know when to stop saying *I am sorry*,
and one day their heart stops of its own volition,
uttering the ultimate apology:

I am sorry I beat too loud. I am sorry if the thuds
made it hard to sleep, I am sorry
and I will stop, Who am I
to claim your precious peace?
Who am I to disturb your life
by asking to have mine?

They don't throw funerals for hearts, bodies
beat senselessly on, machines
composed of flesh, spare parts, and a little
engine grease.

They don't throw funerals for the little deaths
and blank stares, the absence of light
where used to be plenty.

Instead, it is just bodies
crashing on subway trains,
their hearts shameful luggage lying right there
on the pavement
for the whole world to see,
as if to say: *No.*

No,

I have seen it all
and I refuse to be moved.

Hearts leaping out of chests
and laying down, a chorus of no,
no,
nos.
A chorus of: *I refuse.*

Useless things, these hearts
when they refuse the terrors you submit them to,
when they refuse to get up,
when they allow themselves to atrophy,
just muscles left unused for too long.

who am i

to disturb your life

by asking to have

mine ?

Hearts the Size of Texas

An open grave means very little
when our hearts are the size of Texas.
The first time I ever took a bite with the intent of
feeding myself first,
I thought of you.

Heart the size of Texas, when you laughed,
God would laugh with you.

An open grave means very little when it's nothing
to remember us by.
When I die, you can hear me saying these days,
push me off a boat.
Pour tequila after me.
Make sure I've got my cowboy boots on.

These days, grief is hard to come by.
I've got eighty four years of longing to live in my heart,
I am doing all the brave things I imagine you doing.

An open grave means very little when you are erasing
my fear,
showing me where to take a seat,
and when to say: I am going.
I am leaving this place where nothing ever grows.
I am standing up from a table not meant for me,
and using my two hands to craft my own.

They said I lost my mind on a Tuesday,
and took only what I could carry, but see,
it's easy to love someone when they are dead.
The real kicker is coming into their house
and loving their chaos.

So who will come into my house?
Who will love me at my kitchen table, with my knives
and my apples?

An open grave will mean very little if I don't greet death
like you did,
like an old friend,
and take its hand saying: Hey, you.
I've got so many stories to tell you.

The Girl Is On Fire

The girl is on fire.
And by on fire, I mean
the curtains are blazing and the oven is burning.
I mean, there is so much smoke in the room
that all the wolves are howling. I mean,
the front door mat has gone up in flames.
No one will come in clean.
I mean, the girl is on fire
and she has always been on fire
and she doesn't know how to stop burning.

No One's Hera

Body warm,
numbly trucking along
in the days when all the hands were wrong,
days when I'd have torn my heart out rather than
giving it to cold palms,
days when my body closed down,
mind replaying the same old mistakes.

Soft like sea foam, won't you come play with us?

I wanted to grow thorns,
I wanted to be left alone.
I wanted no one to ever lay a finger on me, slapped away
every hand that came to pull on the threads in my hair,
I wanted to stop seeing tears behind the steering wheel,
wanted to stop the ice in my chest, one eye on him,
the other on the dark road.
I wanted someone to open the car door
and let me out.

I wasn't much for empty promises,
I wasn't much for romance -
it ended with them ripping their own wounds open,
and expecting me to sew them back up.

But I'm no one's faultless lover, I'm no one's Hera,
waiting on the doorstep like an animal gone stupid with
love,

waiting on a glance, a kiss, a touch, collecting scraps
to build someone into a better man.
Not the servant. Not pure,
and not ready for anyone's fresh hell to descend to,
brush spring over rotting bodies.

I think the thread came undone in December,
I remember the pouring rain and the melting snow.
Body bruised,
I stared at the world passing me by.

You don't know what you have til it's gone, they say,
but I didn't want
anything I had anyway. Light attracts light,
but moths too,
I should have known.

So all my poems go out to me now,
all my poems go out to feral August dusk,
the stains on my lips,
my own bruises on my hips.

For a moment I thought I was lost,
but no matter what the world sees,
there are still some secrets
I love to keep.

Room II
darkness
D A R K N E S S

Even the best of the crossroads children
have to return to their true nature.
Haven't *you* wanted to pry the darkness apart,
just to see what lies there?

Persephone: ancient Greek, *the bringer of destruction.*

"Power that shoots forth and withdraws into the earth."

- W. Smith -

You Meet Hades in a Dark Alley

You meet Hades in a dark alley and he's got your name
written all over his skin.
The insides of a TV are upturned, and he laughs:
you should see hell these days.

No one knows what to do with all the light.

There is red neon pooling everywhere and you think
maybe you'll cut a deal,
maybe you'll do something so terrible
that the world could never forget it.

I want a ticket out.

You meet Hades in a dark alley and he looks exhausted.
Falls short
of who he is supposed to be.
Your name is burning burning burning across him,
is marking him
yours.

He smiles ruefully and now you're doing what they all do,
You beg.
You barter.
You make yourself a special thing.

You already got it. He nods at your boots,
the god of death is two thousand and his darkness is

nothing
compared to your violence.

Human,
while the rest of us are dead.

You meet a man with your name on his skin and this time,
you smile.

I'm bored anyway. My place or yours?

But you know the answer already.

It's just three pomegranate seeds to stay, he tells you,
but you are hungrier than that.

The Girl Is Not Sorry

Whatever, I'm not sorry for the fire.

Some days I want to be apologetic,
find faults within my heart
like it is not the loudest fucking thing in the room.

I know how to be sorry
but I am really, really not.
You can't fight this atomic energy.

You like my fire licking at your throat,
wax poetic about ash on my fingers
but it is burning me too, like how I
burn incense sticks
and the ghosts always come back.

You think you are enough to hold me
down? *The world*
is not enough to hold me down.

The radio plays summer and I play
adventure with a gap-toothed grin, a stray
picking up strays.

You think my sorrow makes me a stranger?
I am so full of light, I am not
something you keep in your pocket.

You will spend your entire life
catching me across the world,
like how I catch planes in the night.
Every sign will shout: *Canceled.*

You touch me and come away with tan lines,
skin the color of dusk. Do you know
how tired you must be
to fight evil with weak hands
and still win?

I imagine the best thing my parents ever gave me
was a sword.

So forget what I said.
Foreign languages are not homes for the weary,
and all my poems are for wolves anyway –

They can love you good,
but you can love yourself better.

Fever dreams

Dream one

I was so desolate,
wanted to leave all the gates open for the ghosts
just so that something might come in and move me.
I've poured all there was, tired of miracle cures for
illnesses I didn't even have, over-the-counter solutions
hurling me back until I was as windswept as a plain,
until I was the cliff and the raging sea underneath,
the woman - the ghost - haunting my own field at harvest
moon. I needed a wishbone that came with a wish of its
own, my mind was tired of thinking, and my ears
were tired of listening. I could not stay under the covers
anymore, could not walk down the bridge without
burning it down. I was wildly unhappy and yet,
I was wild. Who was I to listen to all those lies and still
offer due respect? The best part I ever played was myself.
The darling princess, soft like sea foam, I had a choice of
words, and gentleness was not one of them.
They spilled milk on me,
they left me out for the wildcats to find,

figuring feral creatures knew each other by the look in
their eyes alone.
Seven days, I mourned.
Seven days, I raged.
On the fifteenth day, I had no more apologies to offer.
My tongue had turned into an animal,
all it was capable of was want.
It was the end of the world and I was wearing a fur coat,
promises as sweet as cherry pie.
I came and got my money's worth. Reborn from the
journey, having returned with wolves to keep me company,
I was asked. But I had traded my tongue for a bluebird.
It might have been February,
but still it sang.

But i had traded my tongue
for a bluebird.
It might have been
February, but still
it sang.

Dream two

I was alone with the honeybees.
Everyone expected plenty from all of us.
I was sent to practice the art of honey,
learning how to be sweet,
even as I turned into the fabled wolf.
Solitude was a nice change of pace. We knew what we were
given to do, and left alone to our small devices.
On the first day, I was stung.
They called it a rite of worthiness. There were no rewards
for swollen tongues.
On the seventh day, they took to using me as a pedestal.
In the right light, they looked like my coronet.
We had too much. We had not nearly enough.
Blueberry jam every morning. By the time there was honey
to taste, I wanted nothing but. Every drop was a miracle.
Every drop was a reward.
I needed very little to survive later.
The whole town gathered to watch me live off of sunlight
alone.

I NEVER KISSED MY DIN E R

GOODBYE

i knew it was time
to come home

of all left i

that was my silver
that was where i
wanted to live

my longing behind

Dream three

I didn't want to exist outside of empty diners at 3am.
They knew me well. The last booth on the right, me and
the other crossroads children. Felt so blown through,
my cheeks were chapped. The waitress knew my name,
and it was *Sweetheart.*
I watched milkshake spill on the pavement outside, but in
here it was mine to savour. My words were foreign, so I
said nothing. I got into a fight with the highway that year,
but the diner chose me in the breakup.
If you drove long enough,
there was this sliver of the highway where two mountains
parted, and you could see the sea.
That was my sliver.
That was where I wanted to live.
But the highway never cared; it only wanted me for my
body and cigarette butts in the sand. When I found lost
fawns in my driveway, I knew it was time to come home. I
never even kissed my diner goodbye, but it knew.
I left all of my longing behind.

Dream four

All the tales are bleeding through.
In the motel room, I am who I want to be,
and I have good company. Wolves at the door.
The couple two doors down. The clerk with a broken heart;
I can't get Jolene out of my head.
The seat sizzles and I drink cherry Coke by the pool,
wolves splashing water on my legs. The couple has a gun
in their glove box compartment, bright red Camaro I want
to press my lips to. They say they are on the run, but
they always ask about my day.
Strange town sweetheart, I dip my toes.
Someone is making a cherry pie.
Someone is making a huge mistake.
They say home can't be a place you pay for, but
every home comes with a price, don't they know?
My teeth are chattering, this whole land is one big folk tale,
steering me away from crossroads and dark deserts.

I'm tired, I say, but the wolves don't know what I mean.

They know tired as a dull ache cured by a good night's sleep.

I'm tired, I say, but the couple doesn't know what I mean.

You don't get tired with your lover, and tired is all my lovers had seen.

I am tired, I say, and the clerk is beyond repair. Begs me not to take his man away, but I am not Jolene.

I figure I should get a move on,

get tired of the vending machine glow, but it's alright here.

The wolves say to leave, but I am not a wolf.

In the dead of night,

I like the cool sheets. I need no one else.

I think the mountains want me here.

I think the desert knows my footsteps.

I think I am alright, as lonely as I am,

as lovely as I am.

Howl

You've been tired
so you've been decaying;
all of the world's miracles
passing you by,
as you sit and wonder
whether your life is even worth saving.

But you should howl at the moon a little,
make the world feel it,
invent your own magic
and make it merciless;
sacrifice everything
that has made you feel hollow.

Chant it until the stars align;
trace the ridge of the wound
you left in your mouth.
Vow to do better.
Again.
Again.

Crossroads

I stand in front of the headlights and
every gear is another chance to run me over
or walk away.

The fact is that the songs don't sound right
and neither do the poems
when I'm composing them on the road.

You're not supposed to have all the answers ready
a due diligent student skipping school
just to smoke under the bleachers,
spitting prophecies like last night's liquor
but what do I know?
I love my asphalt best.

I have it all.
Everything wants me
and I want nothing.

Explain the alchemy in three turns of the key,
explain all the white picket fence corpses,
the 2.5 victories instead of children
and I am still going, never *we*
because there never was any 'we'
and maybe a kid gets to write a poem
that doesn't look both ways
when crossing the road.

I stand in front of the headlights
and I'm hearing the tick of the doomsday clock,
I'm hearing something like a miracle
but there's no way to tell if I'm gonna die
or come alive.

Well, you can't do anything but wait.

Exhaustion Generation

We were pointless
the exhaustion generation and our eyes
rolling into the backs of our heads for adrenaline only,
gambling everything
so that maybe something would stay.

Pointless,
when I drove my car into the wall that day
and grinned, baby
you didn't know what bravery was until you met me
and I smelled like gasoline;
The first thing I ever did was
burn.

Welcome to the children of progressive parents generation,
abandoning school and uploading videos;
passably cute, moderately gorgeous,
we never knew how to form apologies,
who the fuck ever apologized to us?

Our last teen songs will always have you
throwing up roses in gas station bathrooms.

I can be obscene,
can you be worse? I'm looking for a rival here,
for an enemy here,
what a torn up cliche to be loved.

The only thing I know is how to put chains on me
just to break them down.
Never knew if I'd rather have you
under me,
or all that no-servo horsepower.

And it's not that we don't know how to live, it's that
we are dying to.

I saw a girl take a white picket fence once
just to break it over her knee.

I swear I learned how to live that day.

Rest.revel.rejoice

All these images.moving too fast.and I am begging them to
slow down.let me savour.can we get a moment to enjoy the
fruit of our labor.smear it across our hands.let it drip
down our chins.this,what we fought for.this,the trees.
at least the ground, its dirty kisses.at least let us fall.too
fast.what have we worked for,to have no time left
to hope for.too fast.millions of impulses.some cities are
too loud.some people are too angry.have you noticed.is the
earth spinning faster.are we all part flesh part machine.all
these images.we worked for something.moving
too fast.no time left to rest.to.revel.to.rejoice.and i am
begging them to slow down.let us be human with human
needs again.let us come home at the day's end.let us say.
i.did.good.
i.did.enough.
i.need.no.more.

My Blessed Underdog

I am tired of existing. I want to live.

The line is thin, but it is there.

I want to **live** like a damn firecracker,
like the loudest shout in the night, like
the woman screaming from her terrace
with half the neighborhood unable to admit to themselves
that the crazy bitch
might be right.

Well, you can call the cops on my fury,
you can douse it in gasoline,
you can kill me,
but I will never let you eat me.

Where is the girl who was ready to take on the world?
Where was that little bitch with her scraped knuckles,
school yard fights, never an opponent
too strong for her.

I miss her.

See, the two of us know that the trick
to winning when you're the smaller one
is taking the punches
until the opponent wears out. The underdog.

The underdog.

Where is my blessed underdog?
She used to live in my body,
Her voice was all I could hear.

Now, static
interspersed with social media sermons:
here is what you ought to think.
Here is what you ought to feel.
Forget about your heart and soul.
We know what you need.

Well, I'm tired and I want
my underdog back, the girl
who could kick the world's ass.
All bravado, even with her voice trembling.
Where is that girl because I need her now,
and all these excuses for grief are just that -

Excuses.

She was wiser. An adult,
I am now miserable, but I fit in.
A child, I was happy.
Fitting in was the last thing I'd have thought of.

When all of this is over, bridges will burn in my wake.

There is plenty I can take,
just as long as I have myself by my side.

Jack London

Did you stop the arrow with your hand, girl?
Did all the unfocused photos amount to much?

To memories at the end of the road when your heart is
a crumpled map, roadtrip food staining it forever,
and you think: hey,
I might never get the taste out of my mouth,
the bad coffee, the cheap cigarettes,
people caught in passing
who I did not want to stay. Did you see me,
driving down the highway, did you see me,
I was the girl praying in the car.

The sunlight still haunts me
like when we burn incense sticks
but the ghosts are still on the couch. So we learn to stop
looking.

I have been told that divination runs in my family,
despite the crosses on the walls,
and I am trying to figure out for myself why I clench
my teeth
when I know I dreamt this, but I never dreamt you,
you with your sunset hands, you
with your thrashing heart,
we got all of our dreams
and we are still wearing the same old shoes.

We stop looking and start searching,
I say fuck Jack London,
look at my soul searching go.

I don't even sleep on roofs of cars but I am
seeing some kind of stars so maybe it's good. And mud
is good, mud is
progress, or so I have been told,
but my hands still won't stay on the wheel,
my skin is all wrong.

If this time was a feeling it would be
Calima dust collecting in my lungs,
the warning of a hurricane that never comes.

This time would have me wearing a cowboy hat
and chain smoking in the passenger seat,
looking at signs
and realizing that I don't even need to speak the language.

Rules were made for people who could follow them
and I never had a map.

Just a good sense of where I'm going.

Stop Holding Back

Stop holding back.
Your heart is the wrong kind of worn out,
my mouth is all honey.
I am tired of always having to find miracles in the dust,
why can't we ever get something whole?

Listen, these skies are breaking open,
these skies are already bleeding.
We had so many names and second chances,
but we always haunt ourselves in the end.

Stop turning your seams into golden dreams,
sometimes I think we would bootleg good living, too.

Won't you look at these ruins, these apocalypses
that we named beautiful?
We are not a tragedy - we are the exact opposite,
and so we must burn on. When you set fire
to the broken glass, I swear I choke
on the freedom in the shards.

Our love comes with teeth marks and over and over,
I watch you fight yourself
just because you can't stop it from
scarring.

Here for the Hunger

I'm here because I am hungry.

Hungry for affection, hungry to feel cared for,
hungry to yearn, hungry to burn.
Hungry for more than food, hungry for more than words,
hunger like a thing you never noticed before, hunger
like everything you can see.

I need coffee, I need a pot that never runs out. I need spice
to bring tears to my eyes. I'm just looking for a kitchen
full of light.

I want to dip my fingers in all the pies,
I was hungrier than I realize.

Gratitude Practice for Not Breaking Your Teeth More than Twice

Golly gee whiz wouldn't ya know it
it's all good until I am a monster
and then it's not okay because *good*
doesn't come with a baseball bat, *good*
doesn't smash your windows and
steal your gold, *good*
is what I make of it.

It's a new dawn, new definition,
watch me carve good with a sharp knife.
Weaponize my good, a monster
for as long as I'd like, monster
is on everyone's tongue these days
so I take a lover and name it terror,
a synonym for love.

(haven't you
sinned?
don't you
want to do something terrible?)

In my defense, I was carved open.
In my defense, I have been leaking love
ever since I was born.

Good God, what do I do
when I am all salt?

in my defense,

i was carved open

in my defense,

i have been leaking
love ever since i was born

War Goddess with Pigeons Dying Everywhere

Stars,
I have gasoline mouth.

Who

is this hungry?

One night, I stood underneath the neon sky and
  demanded
it give me the future.

It did not say no.

I followed the thread to faraway places,
  rambled and roved until
  all my bones were broken, until
  there was nothing truly mine
  left of me.

Seven days, I mourned.

Seven days, milk and incense.

On the eighth day, I rose.

They saw me in a cage one fine July day,
A war goddess,

                             pigeons dying everywhere.

I wanted to be silent, I wanted
  to be left alone. Tired of words,
  how everyone was using them wrong.

I reek of stardust,
  but my bones are
           Gold.

Mothers hid their sons from me,
birds flocked to the west of my body,
I could not trust myself to be good,
but I wanted what all creatures do.

Won't you help me pick the arrows out of my back?

I write all my poems in a fever now,
I don't explain a single thing -
an animal gone stupid,
there isn't a battle I haven't lost.

Cages

There was more desperation in our actions
than we would like to admit,
how you gripped my hips,
how I gripped the suitcase handle,
how we took our life like sweet pomegranate
and squeezed
until just blood came rushing out.

I was a ripped plane ticket,
one foot on the ground. The other
in the sky,
and I was unfeeling so I let myself
feel it all,
stood in the ocean and let it hit me,
walked away with bruises.

We were more desperate
than we would ever admit -
some things you can tell the world,
others you have to write in code.

These stories will be written in departure
terminals, terminal decisions made
with the world turning away
and maybe I am tired of loud voices,
and maybe I am a step away from breaking
into a new universe,

or maybe every stitch
has fallen apart.

We were desperate,
we were,
so let that pound like we did -

Every hit,

another cage breaking.

Holy Ain't

No one sings
like man does of sinning
but how are you going to see the light
if you don't make peace with your demons?
All that purity led you nowhere,
so you might as well fall to your knees
and come to terms with me.

Holy ain't what holy really is anymore.
Holy is what they made it out to be.

No song like the one of fighting,
taking the punch and asking, is that all you got?
Nothing sweeter than smiling through bloody teeth.

When the bass drops,
when your eyes roll into the back of your head,
forget about the cage. The cage you made
to keep yourself from straying
isn't the temptation.
What you do with your freedom is.

Stop repressing your darkness,
it's you
as much as anything else is.

And the real devil is in licking up the praise
for being a good girl.

Motel Rooms

Room I

God, all the neighbors could hear just how much I liked
you.
For you, I had nothing but honey and sugar,
sweetness for days.

I craved you like I craved all stolen things,
your little death girl, blowing smoke from your palms.
Too many years, still remember it now, the taste of
your skin in my mouth.

I'd have killed for those pearly whites, the grin, wearing
nothing but a smile,
opening the door to let you in.

I forget your name now,
it's better we play dead now,
but I've got a sweet tooth
and your body was my cherry pie.

Room II

I know the Balkans like the back of my hand.
Your hand slips off the steering wheel,
and falls on my knee. Your city's lights,
they shine so bright.
I find an ache stumbling out of my throat,
the first time it was enough
not to want anything.
My legs too long, I don't fit into the curve of your life,
but shit, I still find myself missing squirming in your car,
the night like a confidante. Your city is blind now,
my hands are not kind now, but I miss
the throats bared to the stars. I would give a lot
for one moment of brick wall more.

Room III

I wanted to write lewd poetry. Just downright fucking
dirty, dirtier than you can speak. Take the pretty
cotton candy fantasies and make them mine.
It's half the fun. Taking apart a myth and making it vicious.
So Persephone calls Hades *daddy*. Licks her lips and pops
her p's. His thumb grazes the roof of her mouth so it is
no wonder she chose darkness. Can't compete
with that kind of heat.
Let's make it ours. If you don't tell, I won't tell.
Hit my leg under the table.
Your mother doesn't need to know the kind of filthy shit
we get up to on her vanity table.
Rewind.
Aphrodite fucks strangers for a price and the price is lust.
Twin hunger strangers always have.
If you don't tell, I won't tell.
His mouth tasted like cheap liquor and second-hand
smoke. Did I tell you about the time when I wrapped my

legs around his waist? You called and told me I was wild,
our nights, all feral heat. How beautiful it is
to remember the July fever and not want it back.
This is not a pretty poem and I wonder,
when she kisses you,
does she still taste me on your tongue?

Cherry sweet.

Room IV

All the nights with wet want clawing its way up my throat,
whiskey tobacco ash
moments.
Come on, baby,
I only kiss you because I want the world
to reveal something
to me.

Room V

What a beautiful thing, to be loved as you're growing,
with all of the ugly parts
and cruelty.

What a loving thing to say: "If you need to be cruel
to survive,

then sharpen your teeth on me."

Room VI

Sweet like cherry pie,
come and get your money's worth.

I talked enough sense to lose my mind,
as the song would put it.
Felt so blown through that only an Arctic winter
could cure
what was boiling inside.
I jogged in ports and drank too much and thought
too much and felt very little. *Tired*
pulled me down and held my head underwater.
I was the only person in the sea for miles, and I let it
come over me.
It was saltwater baptism,
every
breath
I
chose to
take.

Room VII

The man who wants my heart tells me: I want to build
a dynasty,
and if my children ruined it,
I would no longer love them.

I sit there, my children and his children and our children
strangely intertwined, so I wonder if he knows
who he is talking to, what kind of woman
is sitting across the table from him.

I would drag myself to hell and back *for my children.*
I'd wreak havoc and cause thunderstorms *for my children.*
Pull the world apart
for my children.
Just like my mother,
I know what responsibility means.

Dynasty?

I imagine my dynasty turning to rot in my child's hands,
and saying: *ruin my life's work,*
baby?

Of course you can.

Just bring a hammer,
I don't want you hurting your pretty hands.
Ruin my life's work, I don't care about
the walls.

I only care about *you,*
               the person I am building them for.

Room VIII

he wants to cut me up, i know it

he wants to

cut me up

and he doesn't

want to

make me

bleed – he

wants to

make me

stop,

which is somehow

even worse.

Room IX

Instead of apologizing,
how about I say this
instead:
I will stop running
when you give me a reason
to stay.

Bird Bones

Always
open the closets
of those
who promise
that *they*
have *never*
buried
a singing thing.

Autopsy

We love out of ultimate need, older than our bones.

I drag my body to your doorstep
just to see you kick me out
and it's alright,
my mouth is full of honey.

We love out of selfishness.

I love how I look in the mirror
with your hands on me;
sometimes I think I am older than myself
full of consuming need.

I offer my mind on the platter
for five cents
to anyone who cares
what is shame anyway?

We perform the autopsy together.

I am the body
guiding your scalpel.

Jimmy part II

Healthy? Healthy is for people
who don't know any better.
Jimmy and I have our own thing, all oil
and nuclear fallouts everywhere.

Sunday afternoon he's bored
so he picks my name out of his mouth,
using my ribs for toothpicks
but nothing in me minds,
everything in me delights.

I love him until we're just flesh and tendons,
until the graveyards know our names, until
we get our money's worth so Jimmy says
open up your veins and bleed.

I say: bleed what?

I was in love once and it broke my bones.
When I leave the house now, I pour salt
over my shoulder, I am all out of things to give.

Every miserable thing I have left is mine
and mine alone.

Seasoning My Heart

i stand at the kitchen table and take a knife
to my heart,
just the way my grandma taught me.

You see a powerful woman going crazy for love and you
think
poor thing,
poor thing, she should know better than to let
a lover
dim her shine.

Why does a woman
seasoning her heart with cilantro
and pimenton
count as mad, when her lover
has his stomach
             full?

What did Frida Kahlo think, I wonder
when she held an ugly man's
ugly heart?
Was it not a nightmare?
And what of the paintings?

Has anyone ever thought
of the paintings?

So what would Frida say,
which words would she use
to explain her choices?

Or would she use none
and burn on?

Those who loved me best
never held my hand
but they knew how to move my heart.

Dying in the Convenience Store

I am dying in the convenience store
and you are telling me that I am too much.

It's a simple scene and I'd laugh
but I am dying, so it's a little hard.

I'd appreciate a hand here
the PA keeps saying the onions
are on sale for 2 euros per kilo and okay, okay,
I know that when the world ends,
it doesn't end for anyone but me,
but you really should have worn socks.

Not that I'm judging you, you have every right
to roll your eyes and spill your heart out
while I'm dying on the linoleum floor.

Shit, I thought I'd get better than that, kinda imagined
a plane crash or something better than this. Olive oil spill
in aisle three, we have opened a new cash register
for our loyal customers.

"Can you listen to me?"

Good question & I absolutely cannot.
Let me explain:

I am dying.

When you come to *my* convenience store
and say to *my* face
that I am too anything (too dramatic, too volatile,
too cold)
why are you surprised when I send you out?

It's not good for me to lock up my dark parts.
You get that, right?

I am not a dumping hole for this world's emotions,
I am not the front door mat
that has to make sure you come in clean.

How could you ever think that my duty to you
surpasses my duty to me?

I am dying in the convenience store and my last view
of this world will be laundry detergent
with a hole in it, the powder
spilling out on the floor.

At least it won't be you.

Death in aisle two, the PA crackles.
Get our fresh tomatoes for just twenty cents apiece!

New Scene, Same Crimes

He says getting lost in me is easy,
take him farther in three days than others do
in a lifetime. He moves to me like a favorite song,
licking rage off my lips. But don't I keep it fun?

No other woman in your passenger seat you'd rather have,
calls me his countess, shows me exactly what he'd do
if he couldn't keep me.

But baby, I love my exit signs, all the shirts you ever wore
stained, they'll feel me on you for years to come.
And isn't it sweet, the shit we did? Isn't it sweet,
closing the door while it's still good? Honey, I love you.
Honey, I am dying for you. Honey, you made me
neon.

And don't mind my hands in my pockets, my eyes
On the watch. I promise you won't feel a thing.
They are calling my name now, another suitcase packed.
You promised you would break me,
but I'm not the one shattering now.

It's a new scene,
but our crimes stay the same.

The Synthetic Violence of a Motel Room Romance

Give me the synthetic violence

of a motel room romance,

the magic in three acts of:

number #1. forgiveness

(you touch me and leave honey;

I wash the blood in the bathroom sink

and the towels smell like your skin)

number #2. carnal

(I look at your collarbones;

how can you trap light, how

can you never let it out – this is magic,

this right here.

That you touch my ribs

and make the flowers grow)

number #3. goodbye

(I'm tired of spitting apologies,

but we've got poison between us

and our house is on fire)

When they ask you where did the light go,
I want you to tell them:
when she takes,
she takes mercilessly.

All night I've been listening to static,
waiting for her to appear.

Summer Rot

If summer was made for anything but rot,
it wouldn't be this scorching hot.

This born-to-die lana-del-rey type of shit,
in which I miss drinking vodka in your shotgun seat,
silk and lace and various states of disarray,
midnight trysts, born without a shameful bone in my body,
lying on your dining table for the whole world to see
what a mess you've made of me.

That summer, I baptized myself with saltwater;
I've grown familiar with motel rooms,
midday sun, your boots when they kick up dust,
screaming up a storm when I was sure no one could hear;
falling asleep anyway,
hopped up on pills and Tanqueray,
as you drove on home.

Literary Sexts
After A. Oaks & C. Siehl

sext: come here. i want to see the laws of physics in action when your hips fall on mine.

sext: your bleeding heart makes my mouth hungry.

sext: we can fuck, but i'd rather peer into every crevice of your mind. did you forget that i know what made you this strong? did you forget what made me this feral? i still remember your childhood tragedies.

sext: today i walked through a museum and i swear every statue carried your face chiseled in the marble.

sext: i remember when you threatened to throw me into the river. for the first time in forever, i was not afraid.

sext: it's so fucking ridiculous – we're both chasing our dreams and we're dreaming of each other.

sext: all i have is this lonely want. how can you believe in stars when they hate us? come here. come here, there is still room for you on my twin size bed.

sext: i hope someone else is kissing your bruises better. they always tasted sweet to me.

sext: i wish we didn't believe in destiny so much. i just miss you.

sext: I have written you a poem so that you may live forever, but my favorite part was when you said that you just wanted to live with me.

sext: drinking wine. thinking how i'd like to drink you in.

sext: i live near the desert but you are making me a humid summer all year long. palm trees everywhere.

sext: i melted for you first.

sext: you make me feel like the 1975 is playing on the radio. every day is midnight at the laundromat; me on the counter, you everywhere.

sext: you are a fever dream and i haven't stopped shaking ever since.

sext: with you, everyone else is just background noise. i hold your words between my teeth and the taste fills my throat.

sext: come here right now. my mouth is so full of missing you that i have forgotten what shame is.

I Do Some Things Louder with You in the Room

My mouth is so empty without you
look – my jaw is clenching on nothing,
there is still love lingering in my cheeks.

I like red on white best
like the time I came out sobbing wet
and you wrapped a towel around my body,
my nails red like they were bleeding across
the white cotton, marking
something that has always belonged to me.

My mouth is so empty without you
look – this hunger makes me do things divine,
there is still a lot of creature left in me.

I was only flying when you were driving,
a fucked up passenger
capable of spouting downright lewd poetry,

but wasn't it fun? Me with my pill smile,
you with your careful eyes.

My mouth is so empty without you,
look – the sky is crying with relief,
it's life set to a luscious beat.

My mouth is so empty without you,
look – this ache is a gateway,
I do some things louder with you in the room.

Four Months

In four months' time
will you think of your mother,
or will you think of my thighs?

I am sorry
for not being sorry at all,
I would have licked the column of your spine,
both of us were searching for something.

Tell me,
did you find it on the train tracks?
No,
I just want to know -
did it feel like blue sky
one last time?

If I say that I feel something
which I cannot name,
will you help me look?

I was so empty and out of it,
I became full again,
like when I swallowed the ocean and said,
I feel like I am *more*.

So put me in the taxi and let me
be shameless again.

So what if cab drivers know what I
whisper, how I giggle, how I find
a hundred ways to show that
yes,

I am respectable in one universe,

but I'm just heat and lust
in this one.

We Are So Good

And I could get drunk on it,
drunk and dance in the middle of the street,
put cracks in the pavement, put flowers, too.

Get drunk on staying up until the sunrise,
drunk with the mad and the dirty and the filthy,
we are *all*
mad and dirty and filthy
but we are good,

God,

we are *so good*
and we have never been happier.

Cotton Burns

Sometimes it scares the shit out of me
when I see the kind of violence you'd like to commit
when you see my baby blues;

Sometimes it scares the shit out of you
when you see the kind of violence I
would like to commit for your hand on my thigh.

If we're being honest, your fantasy of girlhood innocent
is getting off on the same thing;
I love me some cotton candy, white cotton
kind of sweet.

You're not the only one I know with daggers for fingers,
but I like yours best. When you reach inside me and find
barbed wire, razor burn
kind of joy.

Uniquely Singular Ways

Three failed dates and five tequilas later,
it's time we came to terms with the fact that it's always
going to be
you and me, oh sugar oh baby oh
honey,
fucked up in such uniquely singular ways
that no one else could possibly fit.

You know all the right places,
I know all the right excuses.

Imagine us weightless. We take only what we need,
and no one blames us for it. *Red*. You feed me
grapes and watch me eat. Count my bites
for me. *Red*. Our mothers cry when we leave,

You pour love into your children,
and this is how they repay you?
By loving themselves?

We deserve this,
we did enough.

How about we take something too far,
for once in our lives?
I'll bring matches if you bring gasoline,
there is a hunger in my throat that burns bright for you
only.

growing older
growing sharper
all out of awe

Out of Awe

Breaking in the leather of your new sports car
I wonder if speed would taste so sweet
without me in your passenger seat.

These days my teeth are clenching,
my throat is full of want
and they say keeping secrets is good for the soul,
walking 'round smiling like I know something they don't,
but we depend on suspension of disbelief,
we depend on blood and honey;

We love like we are bracing for impact, growing
older and growing sharper,
all out of awe.

Kiss/ll

I would have you kneel for me

and the best part is
I see your eyes
all honey
and you know it
you know it.

And I know that I scare the shit out of you,
I wouldn't have it any other way,
you know I have a head full of
wicked filthy lovely dirty
poetry.

I would have you feeling three lifetimes
and all the pain they caused me
and you would take it because
what is a man to a coliseum,
what is love to what we have?

Here is the thing about broken things like us:
they are always a little chipped
at the edges,
always a little *off,*
and you are a moving set of bad
coping mechanisms
but shit
I have never felt more *seen,*

like you can feel the darkness
like it's a match
to yours,
never
felt
more
seen.

And I would have you kneel for me,
ask how badly it could hurt
is it worse
is it worse
but I would pry the darkness open
just to see
(as always,
curiosity takes the best of me)
what beautiful things we could make,
what havoc we could
wreak.

And it makes me go weak at the
knees
so kneel.

Does it break you open wide,
what does it taste like,
how bad do you want it?

This is not healthy -
sure it's not,

but if it's what we need,
I'd take that fear.

My body is a map of battlefields,
not constellations,
and you've got a pretty mouth,
so why don't we move
because we look like we are about to
kiss each other
kill each other,

And the best part is,

we both know it.

Theatrics: A Not-Quite-Poem in 8 Acts

Let me tell you how I walked six miles
just not to lose someone I could have loved
only to realize there was no love to be found.

Let me tell you how my heart was broken on the highway,
how I wanted to be the deer in the headlights,
wanted to be the stop sign, the speed limit,
the things that would stop him,
wished I could do anything
to stop this trainwreck
from unfolding.

Won't you let the car keep running?
I worry now that it's started,
it's gonna die if we stop it again.

Let me tell you how assholes have told me
they knew better than me
what my words would say,

finding excuses for their pathetic weakness,
trying to put it on *my* front porch,
thinking I would ever be a home
for their shit.

> *I think I did enough*
> *and became enough*
> *to cut myself open,*
> *but never let you dissect me for fun.*

So let me tell you that I'm overflowing
with pent up words,
let me tell you that I'm not sorry for a single "fuck you,"
because goodbyes have always been my favorite parts,
catching planes
with every sign pointing to me an exit sign,
screaming loudly:
We never needed you here.

We always knew just what to do
with our own damn selves.

Wear Red

It starts with gin and pills,
maybe not both at the same time,
but a kind of much needed peace.
I chase the feeling across towns; the calm in my
chest, the sky breaking open with relief.
I exhale,
and the world exhales with me.

I let go of all that I could never
carry.

I crumble into myself.
I take dreams of broken teeth and empty suitcases and
willow branches to weave a nest. It's a small,
shitty, rock-bottom nest, but it's *mine*
and I don't give a fuck:
I love my rock bottom nest.

I dream myself a thousand lifetimes.

In one, I am begging to be forgiven on someone's doorstep.
In another, I am sinking to the bottom of the river
and asking: does this make me pure?
I dream myself books and teak and petrichor and
liquor, I dream myself
a new reflection, one less scarred, please -
(these days I just look at myself like – Oh, this
fucked up thing? I got that in a no man's land.)

I come back to myself and find it all so simple;
where the hell am I gonna go if not up?

I wear red.
I am celebrating something.

In a fit of fury, I leave.
I leave a lot.
Somewhere off the highway, I leave myself too.
I bury her in a shallow grave because I might need her,
and resurrection is so easy
when you know what the ghosts want to hear.

I learn the taste of liminal places intimately.
I smoke too much, I don't drink nearly enough.
Once, I spend a whole month without ever leaving the
house,
like an afterthought.

Like an afterthought, I forget to celebrate
birthdays and anniversaries and lives
boiling in me.
I leave faster.

I buy sturdy shoes and a new jacket and meet
people who say my name the way I have never
heard it before. They hold my name in their mouths
like it is precious, like it is something to
treasure.

a Novel Concept,
and I am not ready.

I take my belly and turn it into a pitcher,
all I do is pour all that I could never say.
When I hit my knee against the table, I scream.
Does it hurt that bad? God, no.
I just have a lot to make up for.

I eat like the cavalry is coming,
wear combat boots
to all the nicest restaurants.
I let myself be nurtured.
I kiss men who... well shit, they're not going to love me,
you know? But we can both agree to love
this moment.

I walk six miles and never even feel a thing.

My heart is strangely quiet.
My heart hears five "I love you"s in a year and
says nothing.
I prod it with my broken nail, say, "Don't embarrass me,
come on, say something, for fuck's sake"
and my heart, the fucker, locks its mouth and
throws the key into the river.

Later, I understand.

Later I say: good on you. At least one of us
is using their brain.

But anyway, at some point
I start wearing red.

And I got this feeling I can't shake-
it's like I am celebrating *something*
but I don't know what it is.

I just know that it is important.

It might be my life.

Girls Dark Alleys Are Afraid Of

I am tired of your morality that only comes out when girls
play with matches and speak in the voices of gasoline.

Yes, please tell me more about your quiet and pretty girls
who stand silently in the face of the apocalypse. Tell me
how their little mouths don't even part.
Tell me about your cotton fantasies,
do they help you sleep at night?

Quiet and pretty girls? No. I know loud girls. Devastating
girls. Wonderful girls. I know girls who refuse to let the
world take something from them. I know girls who fight
with all they've got, and still have some left to spare.

I know furious girls whose survivals are just another notch
to tally up on the bed post. Lovers? Lovers are nothing.
Let them show you how many times they had to learn to
love the world again.

And again.

I know victorious girls, always louder than the rest, baring
their teeth with special pleasure when the world tells them
that they can't. No apology will ever cross their lips.

And I know Icarus girls, too. Those who always chase the
feeling and press their mouths to the world's lifeline.

They know that death is a small price to pay
for becoming immortal.

I've always danced to the tune of myths, stories,
monster girls unashamed of their wildness.

Baring their teeth, turning apologies
into radio static.

The kind of girls
dark alleys are afraid of.

Letters from the Underworld

I'm so bored, mama,
I wanna burn.

Look at me, you've turned a perfectly nice girl
into a feral creature. All I dream of are wolves.
And he's got lips like raw cherries,
he's the lover I demanded all my life,
mouth full of cotton and sugar,
between his ribs, an orchard grows.

He loves me and some nights,
I love him too. Days with him
turn into months of liquor
and honey;
all I do is flow.

Look, he looks and sees. Look,
I'm naked in the most crowded of rooms.
I was your prodigal daughter and my name was
joy. I was the daughter
and I was full of rage.

Now his orchards grow from my heaves,
now I need fire to survive.

Room III

into the fire

INTO THE FIRE

At the intersection of the sun and the moon,
there is freedom
everywhere.

πυρίφοιτος (pyriphoitos): ancient Greek epithet of
Persephone, *walking in fire.*

"Kore, you who've parted the gates of steel unbreakable.

Persephone, o triple-headed goddess, who walk on fire."

- H. D. Betz -

Two Daughters

My mother gave birth to two daughters. One knew
how to sing pretty songs. The other dreamt of
wolves. Good daughters, or so I have been told,
breathe. Good daughters close their hearts.
Good daughters
do not make their blood chant.

Good girls don't want to dissect darkness, stain
their hands with themselves. They eat raw cherries.
Good girls obey. But I wouldn't know obedience
even if it spoke my name.

I don't know how to form apologies anymore. I love
every inch
of my dirty life.

*good daughters
do not
make their
blood chant*

Response to poems and people that would have me broken just because I've been through some shit:

Can you stop? I dragged myself out.

My knees are still skinned. I drew blood

and I fought and fought until it was just

muscle and bone. Can you stop?

I thought of the sun all the damn time.

Can you stop? I have always been

kind and beautiful. No hell

could ever take that from me.

Can you stop? I am not a tragic backdrop,

not a song to sing when your heart is

heavy. Can you stop?

I don't want your hands if you think that

touching me

will make you seem capable of healing.

Can you stop? Heaven is built

through knowing what hell is.

there was barbed wire &

miracles everywhere.

Saints

The saints I have held in my palms
are riding in the backseat of my car
and I can't stop saying I am sorry.

Saint Leopold points out gas stations
all their crooked signs
and St. Jude laughs, doesn't mind -
she likes her coffee cold
and her music loud.

The saints say: dance
so I do,
there is a terrifying need in me
for some miracles that matter.

They don't mind my feet going to all kinds of places,
my grandmother's dusty shelf saints made brand new,
speaking tongues just to say
God is in dirty places, too.

I dug up my heart one night,
we were on mile five thousand and Leopold held the light.

My heart and I,
we made a lovely pair,

There was barbed wire and miracles everywhere.

Fever Year

I spent the year in a fever,
I was walking around like half wishbone half person,
thirsty for something to move me.
I spoke to my loved ones
in a language for which I was missing words.

I dreamt of laying down on the sidewalk
letting the world pass me by,
I dreamt of laying down anywhere,
as long as it was quiet.

And my bones have never been this way, I needed time
to understand what it meant
to be me.

It was the year I turned into a mirror,
I was incapable of holding up anything else
but the truth.
I was feral under the sun, too stubborn to kill.
Spitting knives
and prophecies.

I didn't want to explain a thing.

That summer, I baptized myself in saltwater,
so imagine relief.

Imagine it at the very last moment.

I am on my knees.
I am gasping.
I am alive.

Feral II

I couldn't be good anymore, the sensible child,
spouting wisdom like a fountain, the girl
who always took a step back, the woman who
went quiet for the longest time.
I couldn't be good anymore so nothing
on this green Earth wanted me, or found use
for me. Me, with my fierce joys and shrapnel laughter,
roaming and roaming with a hunger gateway
where a heart ought to be. I was useless to trees,
and birds didn't want me either. I was alone,
not even the air would shift around me. Flesh machine
with renewed vigor, I was a heavy creature
to bear. But I had creature passions, still.
Still wanted to see the break of dawn even if it was not
meant for me, still wanted the tumbling love,
the overflowing orchards, all the sweetness
for me and mine. I took my bones and gave them back,
opened my own throat and said: live.
And I was alone but I was not lost,
the wolf creatures surrounding me, the ground trembling
to uphold me.

Good Hands with No Conversations

My life, a tin can full of bright dreams and good wishes.

My life, like a war that stops at the right moment.

Listen, I am much, but I am all that these bones could ever

hold. I am capable of working magic with just an exposed

bulb, a bottle of whiskey, and a single butterfly bandage on

your bathroom sink. Yes, I would be there at 3am

to close your wounds. I would, and it terrifies me.

My heart, an exposed nerve. The physical manifestation of

leaning across your lap at the drive-through window,

hands all over. My foot on the gas pedal,

I was born to make asphalt burn.

Listen, some nights I can't reconcile myself with you in my

dreams. I was born with a wishbone for a heart, and all it

does is break, break, break. They gave me so much sense,

and I was a perfectly good creature. Look at me now,

gone stupid with wisdom. I just need a silence that won't

look to start a conversation. These hands I have are not

worker's hands, but they can do good work. Honest work.

The kind that makes your heart smile,

makes your stomach full.

And I've always been terrified, surrounded by people who

looked at me and only saw skin around the story.

You can't know until you know;

the immensity of my love frightens me.

For all my pretty poems, I still write in code.

I still look for sunlight.

My God, I am not a tornado,

but I could be the field

it blows through.

Standing with my Fear in the Forest

I was standing in the forest,
and my fear was standing by me.
In the light, it looked unloved. In the light it said:
I never wanted to be this.
My fear is a monster, paranoid hopes made flesh.
I poured and poured, sampled it like iced tea, said:
needs more sugar.
My fear grew
like all unloved things do.
My fear has bad coping mechanisms, my fear does not
know how to hold its own hand. My fear stands shoulder
to shoulder with me and it means no harm. It wants to
keep me safe. I take my fear and turn it into a sword.
See if that makes me easier to carry. My fear
breaks my wrists and says: *I am sorry.*
Who is responsible for me?
My fear is looking for its maker, but everyone
washes their hands clean.
My fear says: *you're all I've got, and not even you*
want me.
I am standing in the forest, and my fear is standing by me.
In this light, I am the perpetrator, not the victim.
In this light,
I am empty of guilt when I say: you are not my duty.
My fear says: *someone*
has to love me. / (That someone will not be me.) / My fear
melts away.
The trees shudder.

Tenderstorm

We had an overflow of supple things,
tenderness kept raining all through January.

We looked for shelter in the wrecks of cars,
poking knees and thighs with cornetto ice cream cartons
like asking, Is this still us?
Do we still have the right to love our ghosts?

You took my hand in that Thelma-and-Louise,
Bonnie-and-Clyde kind of way, a spark lighting up
your eyes, and said: We should make a run for it.

But we are neither sugar, we won't melt,
nor are we cotton candy, leaving sweetness
in our wake.

We had an overflow of soft things that year,
every fire escape in the city was ours.
We lit matches for every wound we encountered,
letting them illuminate what we thought ugly.

When I finally cradled my head, I swear
something sang.

When You Are You

When you are you, you have the most wonderful ideas.
Wake me up at 5am and ask: do you want to go fishing.
We should go fishing. You wear your art like you'd wear
a hat, and I cannot stop laughing. Your hands turn into
wheels, you career to the moon and come back with rocks
in your pockets. We don't have a cat but I imagine it would
feel the same pride, leaving dead leaves on my doorstep:
Look, I can hunt for you. Look, honey,
we both can.

When you are you, you make life a little more worth living.
I am waiting for the moment like waiting for the world to
end. I close my eyes and you start checking the watch.
Can't we stay a little longer? But no, there is the world to
feed, ambition to drive home like a point with cold hands
and shots of espresso. I like you when you are you, our life
is wonderful. I don't even miss being alone. I miss you
whenever you are not around, whenever your hands are
pulled by the dreams or the horses. It's dismemberment,

I'm sure, but you carry it so well until you catch flame and
I have to bring the buckets.

Your mother says to get rest but you can't.
Rest is an illusion, you say when You are not You.
Success is all there is. And I nod, like we both don't know
that in a month's time, you'll fall on my doorstep and
I'll field neighbors' questions like an over-exhausted
PR rep. No, the stray you saw on my doorstep was not me.
No, no, that's a separate woman. I don't know her. No idea.
No, no, no.

When You are not You, we both tire easily. I like us when
we are calm. I like us when we laugh. I don't like us when
the world gets involved. When I am not Me, I spill across
the front door mat. No strength to ring the bell. The
woman who opens the door has my face and the scar on
my lip, when we tumbled headfirst into the side of our
house at six. She says: You Again. I say: Me Again, won't
you let me in?
We've got some rebuilding to do.

Modern Oracle

A new kind of oracle,
giving out prophecies in a bathrobe
like she stirs her coffee
the morning is slow and easy,
but the prophecies still ring true.

Wouldn't you like to be in love?
All you need to know, she says,
is that you don't need to know
all that much.

The key to her heart?

Try looking under the doormat.

You'd like to be smarter? Well,
well, if you'd like to be smarter, you just need
a heart.

And not any heart will do.

And if my heart hurts?

Well, baby,
if your heart hurts,
you need to plant something in it.

If your soul hurts,
you water it twice a day.

So when the hurt comes
you have enough dirt to
~~(blackmail the shit out of it)~~
show the hurt that you're still growing something, so
you may not be ruined at all.

Year and Two Months

My apologies for the delays
I was busy sleeping in airports
getting coffee stains on my teeth
kissing strangers
and laughing.

They don't tell you that €0.25 coffee at gas stations
ends up warming the best,
just like they don't tell you that you'll fall in love with
a 90-year-old jet ski instructor
somewhere off the coast of Africa
just for his passion to live,
just for a second.

When they say you should leave, they forget to mention
that you buy tinsels
and garlands again
and sleep in new beds again,
until every bed feels like your bed,
and you've learned how to make homes
out of pit stops.

My apologies for the delays,
I'm still not sure how to put it into words
that I don't care about filters
(or filter coffee, honestly – *fuck*
filter coffee)
or clapping on planes (I love joy, joy

can stay)
or poetry, really.

I'm not sorry I was gone.
I came alive when I left.

What is poetry to my hands on the stick shift,
boots on the dashboard,
miles of open road?

What's poetry to getting up every day knowing that
nothing's certain but hey,
I have these bones today,
I have these hands today,
and I have this heart today.

They're the only things I've ever packed, anyway.

Sleeping with my Fight

Perhaps it is time to learn the art of soft resignation,
I have been waking up next to a fight in my bed for years
and now there are no more enemies left to defeat.

These days, I look at the moon,
she nestles low
and suddenly I am overcome
by this ancient thing, this deep
deep
exhaustion,
pulling me into myself
until I am so tired that
I don't want to fight anymore / I just want to *be*.

Art spills out of me, leaks
through my fingertips and I can't stop apologizing,
even the people in the street can smell it -
it rushes like my fight once used to
and never comes home before it's time
to wash her knuckles clean.

I open the tap and let the water spill
across my palms, the moon
brushes my hair and if I try,
I see her in the dining room
a pair of kitchen shears in her hands
snip snip snipping away -
all that hair on the floor.

If I try hard enough, I can remember
the magnet in my stomach, the gravity
where I think my soul should be,
pulling me in into myself.

I am not ancient, but I am tired,
so maybe there are lifetimes
beyond this one.

When my anger comes,
I let it fight
but mostly she watches, seethes,
tells me in a shitty bar downtown
that she's had enough of this, asks
whether there's anyone left to fight.

And I could lie to her,
name ten suspects off a list I assembled once
but we pour another one.

See, my anger wants to see Bali,
maybe found a startup,
she's not sure yet,
and I'm looking at her boots on the table,
imagining my neighbor coming out
and telling him that I am going to watch the moon
so he can go back the fuck inside.

Fears stir in the morning
so the fight comes back
and she half-asses it, hair still salty

from another day's swim
asks: is this good enough?

Neither of us want to be doing this anymore.

Tonight, I look at the moon,
she nestles low and the stars rise high.
If I try, I can imagine her going to sleep
so I turn off the heater and pull out a chair.

I do not cut my hair,
but I do not look at myself either.

I grow lazy,
I grow heavy and
sated,
let all this weight pile up,
let the electricity go out,
and thank God for a little less light -
I seem to be finding it everywhere else.

Soft resignation, I tell myself and wash my feet,
tune out the audience in my head.
Inside me, I realize,
there is a soft place
surrounded by thorns,
and every smashed glass,
every gunshot,
sounds like the fight's boots
walking away.

Junkyard of Past Lives

I open my closet, and it's a junkyard of past lives,
jacket versions of myself that no longer fit.
What's wrong with that? Soft.
What's wrong with this? Sharp.
I speak a language for which I am missing words.

I take off my clothes like shedding skin,
step out of a life into a new one.
Sadness could never do.

Scrapheap, I assemble new stories.
Not happy unless it's perfect,
unless I can make it a lesson,
not just a good life,
lived well, worn in like a pair of beloved shoes.
Practical things? I am not a practical thing,
I believe in magic.

I imagine I am holding court,
everyone is asking me who I want to be,
and I, like the duchess of impossible things,
laugh.

I take off my clothes like shedding skin,
only to remain in mine. I've always a needed a big closet,
the best part I ever played was myself.

Rise

I'm not great
at a great many things; I forget
to unpack until I am left shivering
on the hardwood floor.
I stay quiet
when I ought to speak, blaze
when I should simmer.
I don't go to sleep until dawn breaks,
and the guilt of seagulls carries me to bed.

But I can flip pancakes like a motherfucker
(even though I'd never tell you that),
I once ran four miles
just to say I was sorry,
I would serve my heart on a silver platter
to feed the people I love, and
between grief and joy,
I always pick the worst joke. I know
how to unbreak my legs and always,
every single time, without fail,
rise.

I Lost My Grace to Joy

[i'm all naked skin, messy hair, thirsty heart.]

i am an evening dress, bare feet and a bottle of wine by the sea. i am glitter turned sea foam. i am smudged lipstick and sloppy kisses and loving so deeply that you have lost all grace. i am a naked wild dance and smashing plates, a heart that is a war drum, watch me burn, watch me create.

i am feet on the dashboard, endless car rides and roadtrip food, looking at your reflection under a crackling fluorescent light of a gas station. i am the thorns you have to get cut on before you can get to the stars. i am a liminal space, i exist and i don't, pieces of my soul scattering in the wind, sunlight hiding under my skin.

i am so much that my heart breaks, it overflows.
i have never known how to be a puddle when i am the sea.

i am so much that
my heart breaks.
it overflows.
i have never known
how to be a puddle
when i am the sea.

Nights that Slip to Heaven

I'd like me some weird ass trip summer night kind of love
that gets me pulling on my stitches. You are a ragdoll
and I like to envision my bones as a hurricane but when
we close our eyes, we are back under the yellow lights and
your fingers slip down my skin.

What I am trying to say is that I wanna
come away with the wind and your hand rolled cigarettes
are already drying but you fit between my thighs
like a long lost puzzle. This pristine clean
never looked good to me, I loved you dirty.
You are the pavement and you are the mirror,
when the rain comes down and we don't feel a thing.
My legs hurt but my heart doesn't weigh a thing.
I was so tired of carrying it around like a broken suitcase.

I would kiss you even with blades in your mouth
but not mine, oh God, never mine. I could never
do that to you.
You are a fork in the road and you are a wishbone,
I would break you in two 'til there's only longing left.

These days the sun is an oil spill and these days our hands
are paintbrushes – I am tired of nights long and dark,
I'd like them lit up like floodlights. So drop the fight, won't
you? I promise to leave mine on a stranger's doorstep.

We've been creating miracles out of defeats for too long,

I can still hear you saying: *I loved her like a split lip,*
I loved her like cracked glass. Every mile was a forgotten
promise, our fury beating inside us like a second heart.

But some nights slip to heaven so easily and it seems to me
that tonight, despite the dark,
we are one step closer to sun.

Stir Milk and Honey

We're a moving set of bad coping mechanisms, you buy
succulents and I brew kombucha, but at the end of the day
you'd rather reach for pills, and I'd rather reach for thrill.
They say neurons are to blame. Fight or flight is like a
drug, you get used to it. Never know what to do with your
hands unless your teeth are bleeding. But hey, hey,
I don't want to live like this. I don't want to end like this.
And my body is weary, my body is growing soft and heavy,
bones melting into the earth, listen - why don't you come
over here, we could stir milk and honey over my fireplace,
we could lick the sweet off our fingers.

We could live.

Lighter on Our Sins

I don't think God would judge me for lighting up.
I don't think God has the time to judge.
Like all the best creatures, he simply does.

What use is anything else?

I talk and talk and talk
and it just wears me out. You
philosophize, and?
At the end of the day, all our decisions
are made by other people.

Look how little we can control.
Nothing but our small lives.
What is there to live for?
Afternoons with people we love,
sunlight caressing your skin,
poems and stories and cups of tea.

I used to care for someone who was going to leave me
for the revolution.
Three years later, he's still in his home town.

Maybe God wouldn't have judged me
if I'd made mistakes a little more often,
if I sinned just to get a taste of life.

The truth is this: we are okay.
Maybe we're all dirty,
maybe we're all fucked,
hungering for more than we can handle.

But we should all be lighter on our sins.

am i just ExHAustEd now,
the only poem i could
ever write would be

{SiLENcE}

Swallows

I am mink, silk scarves, French perfume now,
looking from the outside in,
praying to God and saying: Imagine if this
was the only thing you had.
And I am just exhausted now,
the only poem I could ever write would be silence.
The trees. The silence. The touching down
of an exhausted bird saying,
I have travelled so far.
Won't you give me your doorstep to lay my head on?
Won't you give me your lap to place my feet in?
Won't you cradle me?
There is so much to look forward to,
and I am tired of being a swallow.

A Simple Life

Like a foal that has forgotten what she was born to,
I have to relearn the practice of walking.
Born to the moon and my immense stars, I learn
how to drift like a pine needle
in the middle of the highway.
I know, tomorrow always brings something new,
but I watch my foal legs and despite myself,
I get excited.
Look, I have done this a thousand times,
but my odds have never been this good.

Rivers and Oceans

Do the Danube and the Adriatic ever meet?
For you, they did.

The sanctity of ourselves is only found
in the people we love,
not in the things we are willing to do for ourselves,
but in the things they are willing to do
to make us happy.

There is a place beyond where nothing
will bother us much
so while we are here, let's enjoy the chills. The thrills.
Let us say "no" to nothing, and bite into every slice of life
like it is our very last,
like this juice coming down your fingers now
is the last thing you will ever taste.

Winter Blues

Summer has fed me well,
so I greet the winter full. For the cold,
I don't even leave my bed. Against summer,
I struggle. For winter, I melt.
It says: leave your ambition behind. Come,
rest. Come, feel. Come,
touch.

Winter is the best lover I have ever had,
he invites me to see what he sees:
Come on, taste. It's not sugar,
but it sates.

Winter says a lot without ever
showing skin. He demands nothing,
takes freely. Winter teaches me
to feed myself first.

Now, winter blues is a thing of the past.

The wind still howls, but now it beckons:
don't stop for me. wear Red,
you have plenty left to celebrate.

Cravings

In this economy, smiles are hard to come by
but my baby's hands are full of me
and I don't even feel like getting philosophical anymore,
I'm so well fed.

And I love the way my baby moves, love
the sacred
and the profane.
I can't trust myself to be good anymore,
but my baby loves me dripping in gold
so the last poem I ever write will be the taste
of mint toothpaste, morning, orange juice.
All delight everywhere that saved me,
no matter what the preachers say.

Used to hold on to sanity,
And now I have cravings,
hunger for days.

Persephone in a Motel Room

Persephone sleeps alone in a motel room
she's got neon painting her face
all kinds of red
like when her mother said
if you leave now,
you don't get to come back,
and her cheek stung for days.

Leaving is much
easier to do
than they tell you.

Persephone sleeps alone in a motel room
and she's got a pretty face,
thighs that don't touch
the only things that chafe is how
she has to grow up now
and it's not easy.

She's got a lover whom
she does not call a lover
spills the dirty poetry into his ear,
it's the modern way
for a very old goddess,
and her tale is as old as time.

The darling star,
no longer interested.

The girl leaves the suburbs behind
all that good advice
deconstructing in flames,
and for that the world wants her broken
spilling across the front porch,
coughing up blood
on the welcome home mat.

But she's got no use for shame,
they don't teach you that at birth.

Now, Persephone wakes up feeling wanted,
impossible warmth turning her belly into a pitcher,
pouring honey all over.

Crave more?

Visit **lanarafaela.com** and join the mailing list to receive 10 more poems, as well as plenty of other exclusive materials.

Thank you for reading, and please, remember:

I. Feed yourself first.

II. Wear red.

III. You still have so much to celebrate.

ABOUT THE AUTHOR

Lana Rafaela Cindric is still on the road, kicking her feet up in motel rooms at the end of a long day.

You can read more of her work on lanarafaela.com, or follow her on Instagram: @lanarafaelapoetry.

She published her first poetry collection about healing and growth - *This Is How You Survive* - in 2017. *Persephone in a Motel Room* is her second book, and she is currently working on her first novel.

She still wears plenty of red.

Printed in Great Britain
by Amazon

46354892R00098